A MONEY ADVENTURE

EARNING, SAVING, SPENDING, SHARING

Neale S. Godfrey

The One-and-Only Common Cents Series ™

Illustrated by
Randy Verougstraete

Silver Press
Parsippany, New Jersey

To Mom, who gave me my best training.
With love from your overachiever, Neale

Special thanks to Rudie, Remie, and Suzanne for all of your loving support.
Randy Verougstraete

 Published simultaneously by Silver Press and Modern Curriculum Press,
Divisions of Simon & Schuster.
299 Jefferson Road, Parsippany, NJ 07054

Design/Cover by Michelle Farinella

Printed in Mexico
1 2 3 4 5 6 7 8 9 10   00 99 98 97 96 95

Library of Congress Cataloging-in-Publication Data
Godfrey, Neale S.
A money adventure: earning, saving, spending, sharing/by Neale S. Godfrey:
illustrated by Randy Verougstraete.
p. cm.—(The one and only common cents series)
Summary: The GreenStreet$ Kids find out how money is earned, saved, spent, and shared.
1. Finance—Juvenile literature. 2. Money—Juvenile literature.
3. Small business—Juvenile literature. [1. Money. 2. Money-making projects. 3. Business Enterprises.]
I. Verougstraete, Randy, ill. II. Title. III. Series.
HG173.8.G63   94-45103   332.4—dc20   CIP   AC
ISBN 0-382-39112-8 (LSB)
ISBN 0-382-39113-6 (JHC)
ISBN 0-382-39315-5 (PBK)

For each book that is sold,
Simon & Schuster Education Group
and the author of this book,
Neale S. Godfrey,
along with Children's Financial Network,
will jointly contribute 25¢ to
the U.S. Committee for UNICEF
to help children around the world.

United States Committee for
 unicef
United Nations Children's Fund
333 East 38th St., New York, N.Y. 10016

It was the first day of summer.
Everyone in the town of Green$treet$
was outside enjoying the day.
The Green$treet$ Kids wanted to do
something fun, but they just didn't know what!

3

Penny Bright,

Dollar Bill, better known as Buck,

Hedge,   Small Change,

Short Cut, and

Ona Budget

were sitting on a bench, watching people go by. They were trying to come up with something to do.

"I know what we can do. Let's tell jokes," suggested Small Change.
"I have a good one: What is the cheapest boat you can buy?"

"I give up," said Buck.

"A sale boat,"
giggled Small Change.

"Let's get serious now,"
said Penny.
"What else can we do?"

5

Buck jumped up and yelled, "I have an idea! Why don't we start a business?"

"What kind of business?" asked Hedge.

"We could make mud pies!" shouted Short Cut. "I can make a great mud pie."

"I don't think people will buy mud pies," said Penny. "Any other ideas?"

"Hey! I have a good idea!" cried Ona.
"Let's sell frozen fruit pops.
They're easy to make."

"That sounds like fun!"
shouted Small Change.

"We could set up a fruit-pop
stand right here in the park," said Penny.
"We could call it
KID Pops—**K**ool, with a K,
                    Icy, and
                              Delicious pops.
All those in favor of the KID Pops
business, raise your hand."

7

"Okay. How do we start?" asked Hedge.

"First we have to shop for everything
we need to make the pops," said Penny.

"Then we have to make the pops.
And don't forget, we need to build a
fruit-pop stand, too," Ona reminded them.

"That's a lot of work!" said Short Cut.

"Not if we all help.
After all, it's our business!"
said Buck.

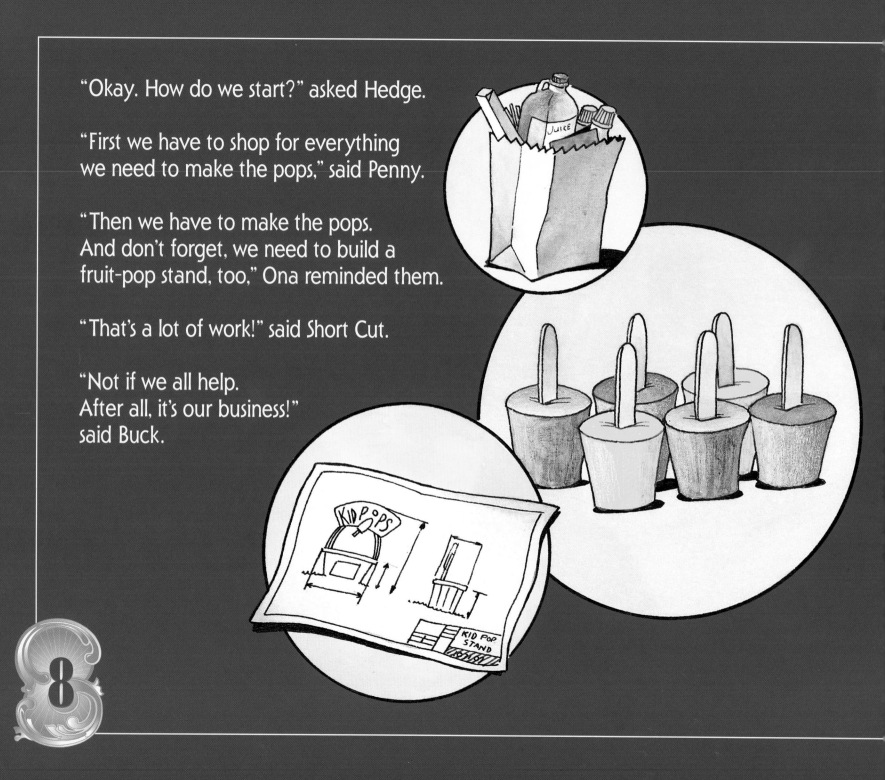

"We need money to buy supplies for our new business," said Ona.

"That's right. We need to invest in our business. It takes money to make money!" said Penny.

"Let's put our money together to buy what we need," suggested Hedge. "If we each give a dollar, we'll be off to a good start."

"Don't forget the fruit-pop stand," Ona reminded them a second time.

"We can use the wood from my old lemonade stand," suggested Buck.

"And I've got cardboard at home for making signs," said Short Cut.

"Yippee! We'll be selling KID Pops in no time!" shouted Small Change.

11

The Green$treet$ Kids began their business that day.
Buck and Short Cut took the list and went shopping
at Bull and Bear's store, the Blue Chip Deli.
Meanwhile, Penny and Small Change worked on building the stand.
Ona and Hedge started painting the signs.

12

The Green$treet$ Kids worked all day.
Before long, the stand was ready for business.
All they needed now were fruit pops and customers.

13

Bull and Bear wanted to help the Green$treet$ Kids make their first batch of fruit pops.
So late that day, all the Kids gathered in the kitchen of the Blue Chip Deli.

KID POPS RECIPE

(Ask an adult for permission before making KID Pops.)

THINGS YOU NEED:

Fruit juice (any flavor)
Small paper cups
Rulers
Scissors

Plastic wrap
Rubber bands
Wooden craft sticks

1. Pour the fruit juice into each paper cup.
2. Cut the plastic wrap into $3\frac{1}{2}$ inch squares. Cover each cup with a square. Use rubber bands to secure the plastic wrap.
3. Poke a small hole in the center of the plastic wrap with the craft stick. Push the stick through the hole and into the juice.
4. Set the cups on a level surface in the freezer. Freeze overnight.
5. To eat, tear the paper cups away from the pops. Enjoy!

The next morning the Green$treet$ Kids were ready for their first day of business.

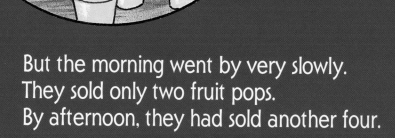

I hope we sell a lot of KID Pops today!

But the morning went by very slowly.
They sold only two fruit pops.
By afternoon, they had sold another four.

How can we sell more pops?

16

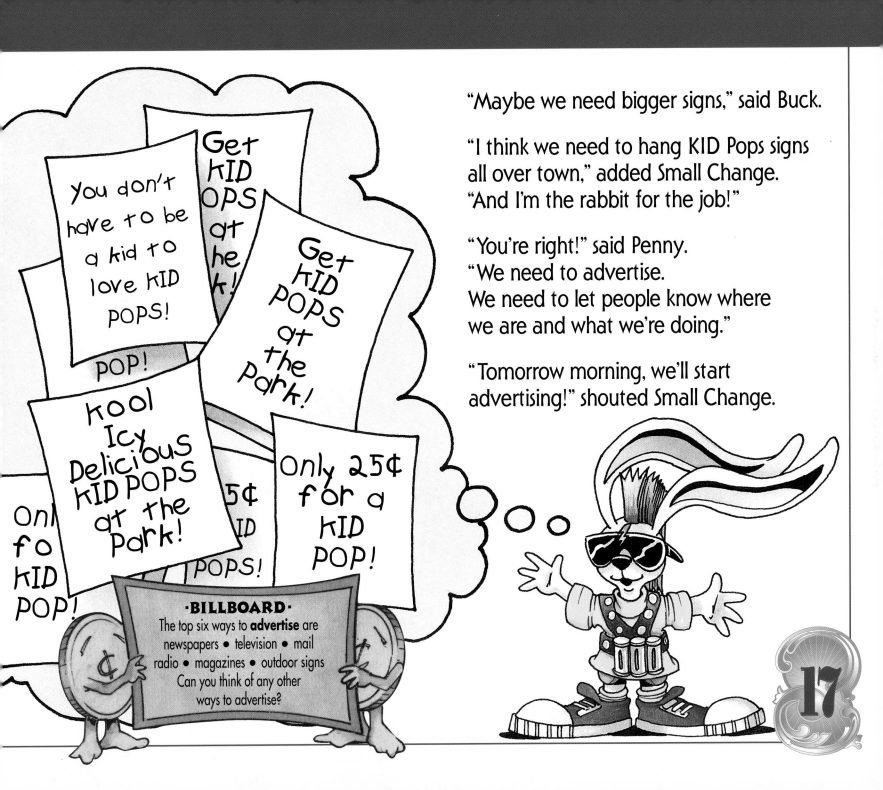

"Maybe we need bigger signs," said Buck.

"I think we need to hang KID Pops signs all over town," added Small Change. "And I'm the rabbit for the job!"

"You're right!" said Penny. "We need to advertise. We need to let people know where we are and what we're doing."

"Tomorrow morning, we'll start advertising!" shouted Small Change.

·BILLBOARD·
The top six ways to **advertise** are newspapers • television • mail radio • magazines • outdoor signs Can you think of any other ways to advertise?

17

"Meanwhile, let's figure out what to do with the money we've earned," said Penny.

The Green$treet$ Kids decided they would count the money they earned that day and share it fairly. Penny divided the money into six equal parts. Ona, Hedge, Penny, Buck, Short Cut, and Small Change each received 25¢.

"What are you going to do with your money?" asked Ona.

"I'm going to save my money to buy a computer," Penny answered. "What about you?"

"I want to buy a soccer ball," said Ona.

"I'm going to buy ten ice-cream cones!" added Short Cut.

"I'm saving to buy my mom a birthday gift," said Hedge.

I want to buy a bike.

I'm going to buy new sunglasses.

·BILLBOARD·
Did you ever save money?
Where did you keep it?
Saving money means putting it somewhere safe so it can be used later.

19

"I know what we should do," said Penny.

"You always do!" said Short Cut.

"Let's go to the bank and visit Banker Bee.
She can help us open our own bank accounts.
Then we can save the money we earn
until we're ready to spend it,"
explained Penny.

The Green$treet$ Kids closed
the stand for the day and
went off to the bank.

"Hi, Banker Bee," said Penny. "We would each like to open a savings account."

"Give me your name, address, and the money you wish to deposit into your account," said Banker Bee. "Then I'll give you a passbook to keep track of how much money you have in the bank."

Banker Bee helped the Kids open their savings accounts. The Kids left the bank with their passbooks in hand, feeling very proud.

·BILLBOARD·
The first bank in the United States opened in 1781 in Philadelphia.

21

Before opening the stand the next morning,
the Green$treet$ Kids were busy advertising.
Penny, Ona, Hedge, and Buck painted
lots and lots of KID Pops signs.
Small Change and Short Cut hung the signs all over town.

Advertising really made a difference.
At the end of the second day, the Green$treet$ Kids
had sold three dollars' worth of pops.

Ona divided the $3.00 into six equal parts.
The kids closed the stand and ran off to the bank to make their deposits.

"Look, here come the Green$treet$ Kids again," said Banker Bee.
"Business must be good."

"We had a great day, Banker Bee," said Buck.
"We sold twice as many KID Pops today as we did yesterday."

25

On the third day, the Green$treet$ Kids sold seven dollars' worth of pops.

"That's a lot of pops," said Small Change.

"But we don't have enough juice to make any more pops," said Ona.
"We need to buy more fruit juice."

"Why don't we use some of our fruit-pop money?" suggested Buck.

"Let's take $4.00 to buy more juice. Then we will still have 50¢ each to put into our savings accounts," explained Penny.

They went off to the bank to deposit their money.
On their way home they stopped at Bull and Bear's store to buy juice to make more fruit pops.

27

It rained all afternoon on the fourth day. The Green$treet$ Kids only sold six pops.

"We didn't make much money today," said Buck.

"No, but we didn't know it would rain," added Ona.

28

·BILLBOARD·
Do you know any money sayings?
"Save for a rainy day."
"Money doesn't grow on trees."
"A penny saved is a penny earned."
What do you think these sayings mean?

"I didn't know that weather could affect business," said Hedge.

"Gee, being in business is risky!" added Small Change.

"Let's deposit our money in the bank and go back to my house and play," suggested Short Cut.

·BILLBOARD·
Risk is the chance you take in business. You may make money or lose it.

29

The fifth day was sunny and hot.
It was a perfect day for selling KID Pops.
The Green$treet$ Kids sold a whopping
36 pops and divided the money evenly.

"We made a lot of money this week.
We could each donate $1.00 to the Pool
Fund," suggested Penny.
"Then we'd be helping our community
pay for the pool."

"With our help, maybe the pool
will be ready sooner," added Small Change.

"Yes, and if we make our business grow,
we can give even more money to
the Pool Fund," said Buck.

POOL FUND

$
$ GOAL
$
$
$
$

·BILLBOARD·
When you **donate** money, you
give it to a good cause.
You can also donate clothes, toys,
and even your time to help others.

POOL CONSTRUCTION

"I've got an idea for making more money," said Ona. "Let's create a brand-new pop. How about Pizza Pops?"

"Could we make Taco Pops, too?" asked Hedge.

"What about Chicken Pops?" added Small Change.

"Now that we know how to earn, save, spend, and share money," said Penny, "we can do anything! Let's get ready for our next money adventure!"

I've had Chicken Pops. They weren't so great.